NCCL

Echoes of Faith™

CATECHIST FORMATION

DIRECTOR'S MANUAL

Edmund F. Gordon
Carol Augustine
Gloria Reinhardt

Project Director
Diane Lampitt

Project Editor
John L. Sprague

Contributors
Mary Braitman
Sister Rosalie Digenan

NATIONAL CONFERENCE OF CATECHETICAL LEADERSHIP

RᴄL

RESOURCES FOR CHRISTIAN LIVING™
Allen, Texas

NIHIL OBSTAT
Rev. Msgr. Glenn D. Gardner, J.C.D.
Censor Librorum

IMPRIMATUR
† Most Rev. Charles V. Grahmann
Bishop of Dallas

September 10, 1999

The Nihil Obstat and Imprimatur are official declarations that the material reviewed is free
of doctrinal or moral error. No implication is contained therein that those granting the Nihil
Obstat and Imprimatur agree with the contents, opinions, or statements expressed.

Design: Dennis Davidson

ACKNOWLEDGMENTS

Scripture quotations are from the New Revised Standard Version of the Bible, copyright
© 1989 by the division of Christian Education of the National Council of the Churches of
Christ in the USA. Used by permission. All rights reserved.

Excerpt from the English translation of the *Catechism of the Catholic Church* for the United
States of America copyright © 1994 United States Catholic Conference, Inc.—Libreria
Editrice Vaticana. Used with permission.

Send all inquiries to:
RCL • Resources for Christian Living ™
200 East Bethany Drive
Allen, Texas 75002-3804

Toll Free   800-822-6701
Fax   800-688-8356

Printed in the United States of America

#13226   ISBN 0-7829-0965-5   *Catechist Formation*

1 2 3 4 5   03 02 01 00 99

CONTENTS

CATECHIST FORMATION

by Ed Gordon

THE IMPORTANCE OF CATECHIST FORMATION

As a DRE you have many responsibilities. No responsibility is more important than the formation of catechists. In 1997 the Roman Congregation for the Clergy issued the *General Directory for Catechesis* (GDC). The document captures much of the Church's renewed under-standing of catechesis since Vatican II. The formation of cate-chists is one area of particular emphasis. The GDC addresses the pastoral care of catechists and lists several tasks necessary for their care and growth. The GDC then says, "All of these tasks are born of the conviction that the quality of any form of pastoral activity is placed at risk if it does not rely on truly competent and trained personnel. The instruments provided for catechists cannot be truly effective unless well used by trained catechists. Thus, the adequate formation of catechists cannot be overlooked by concerns such as the updating of texts and the reorganization of catechesis" (#234).

The writers of the GDC are stating what every director of religious education and catechetical leader knows. The catechetical ministry rests on the shoulders of parents (who are the first catechists) and catechists. It is when the "door closes" or when the child, youth, or adult goes home that catechesis, the communication of the Gospel message, takes place. Every DRE and principal knows this and sees it as a most important and formi-dable task. The GDC says that we must give "absolute priority to the formation of lay catechists."

As good educators, we know that the first step in the learning process is to "know your learners."

Who are the persons who are coming forward as catechists today? By and large they are the parents of children entering our catechetical program, or in the

Truly, to help a person to encounter God, which is the task of the catechist, means to emphasize above all the relationship that the person has with God so that [he] can make it [his] own and allow [himself] to be guided by God.

GENERAL DIRECTORY FOR CATECHESIS (GDC), 139

case of Catholic schools, young teachers graduating from secular universities. Some commentators call this younger generation, Generation X or Gen X. It is the "twenty and thirty something" age group. They are the first generation to come to adulthood in the post-Vatican II Church. They are also the generation to reap the whirlwind of the great sociological and cultural upheavals that began in the sixties.

So what is the profile of the potential new catechist? As in the past, catechists are predominately women (85%). Unlike their predecessors, these women work in jobs outside of the home. The time they can give to formation is limited by family and work obligations. Yet, this is the generation that sociologists tell us is a very different breed of Catholic than their parents and especially their grandparents.

Tom Beaudoin, a leader of a Gen X ministry in Boston, gave the following snapshot of the generation:

- They were all born after the Second Vatican Council.
- Endless politicization around key issues (abortion, birth control, women's ordination, and others) marked the Church's public life during their growing up.
- No significant cultural event in the life of the generation has given impetus or served as a litmus test for them to define their Catholic identity, for or against.
- The most public representative of the entire Catholic Church has been Pope John Paul II. Many Gen X-ers, for better or worse, take him to be the summation of the tradition.
- Latchkey childhoods are common.
- Deep immersion in pop culture.
- Experience of divorced or blended families.
- Computers are their second language.

> The young adult Catholic is Catholic in a very different way than previous generations.

These experiences, both cultural and religious, have shaped a very interesting generation of young people who are becoming our catechists.

Recent social science research yields some challenging data. In many areas they are like previous generations. In a recent survey, the majority of Catholics twenty to thirty-nine years of age responded that belief that Christ is really present in the Eucharist, that God is present in the sacraments, charity to the poor, and the importance of Mary are all essential to the Catholic faith. As one commentator pointed out, "How Catholic can you get?"

Edmund F. Gordon is Secretary of the Department of Christian Formation and Director of Religious Education for the Diocese of Wilmington, Delaware. He also represents the National Conference of Catechetical Leadership (NCCL) as Project Director for the Echoes of Faith *catechist formation project. He is a past president of NCCL, and presently serves on the Steering Committee for the International Forum on Adult Religious Education. A former high-school teacher, youth minister, and parish director of religious education, Ed is the author of numerous articles on religious education and speaks internationally on theological and catechetical topics. He holds a master's degree in Religious Education from Catholic University, Washington, DC.*

On the other hand, there are many signs that the young adult Catholic is Catholic in a very different way than previous generations. Most studies show that the younger generation:

- Is suspicious of any institution, including the Church.
- Does not think or feel that one has to attend Mass regularly to be a good Catholic.
- Makes a rather sharp distinction between God's law and Church law.
- Is relatively uninformed about Church teachings.
- Lacks a good grasp of Catholic vocabulary and speaks in more generic Christian terms.

Some have described this generation as the Christian Catholics! No strong institutional affiliation coupled with a lack of knowledge of the Church's teaching leaves plenty of room for a "generic, cultural Christian" identity to emerge. What we want and need for catechists are strong, Catholic Christians!

As you read this, you might be thinking, "these are not my young adults." It may be true, but remember this axiom: "Your experience a trend does not make." Certainly not everyone between twenty and thirty-nine will exhibit all the characteristics described above. They are, however, discernible outlines of a generation, the generation from which our new catechists will come. If even some of the information emerging from the sociological studies of the generation of young adults is correct, then catechist formation becomes all the more important. How are we going to take a generation on the go and help them become competent and confident catechists?

CATECHIST FORMATION . . . TO BE OR NOT TO BE, THAT IS THE QUESTION!

So now you know who your new catechists are. You know that the catechist is critical to the life of a good parish or school religious education program. You are aware that all the video equipment, the environment, age appropriate textbooks, and teaching aids are secondary to the trained catechist. Yet, all too often, things get in the way of the best intentions to train your catechists. Even if a catechist has a living, active faith, it does not automatically mean she/he has the basic skills necessary for effective catechesis. Nor does good will insure success. So why is it so hard to have a parish catechist formation program?

We have experienced a real community building with those gathered. Since it has been inter-divisional, not all the catechists knew each other except by face. The group felt it was convenient, comfortable, and inviting to have this in our parish. They felt they would not have opened up as much in a new situation.

MARY ANN ROHR, DONNA RAFAELI,
MARILYN SCROOPE MAHONEY,
CATECHISTS
ST. BERNADETTE PARISH
SEVERN, MD

Go, therefore make disciples of all nations; baptizing them in the name of the Father, and of the Son and of the Holy Spirit, teaching them to observe all that I have commanded you.

MARK 28:19–20

Carol Augustine is the Director of Religious Education for the Archdiocese of Baltimore. Prior to her diocesan work she served as a Catholic school teacher and parish Director of Religious Education. She holds a bachelor's degree from Mt. St. Agnes College in Baltimore, Maryland, and a Master of Education degree from the John Hopkins University.

Take a few minutes to reflect on the following statements.
Check any statements that may be true for your situation:

You as the DRE/CRE Catechetical Leader have said the following:

____ I already wear too many hats—my job is already two full-time positions!

____ How can I fit one more program into my schedule?

____ The catechists don't come. They do not have the time.

____ The catechists do not want content.

____ My catechists only like the "how to" training with lots of handouts.

____ I spend all my time recruiting. I am lucky I have a catechist for each class.

____ It is hard to design a program because of the catechists' varied background and interest level.

____ I do not know how to design a program to meet the needs of the Gen X Catholic (under thirty-five).

____ I do not know how to fit a catechist formation program into the catechist's, parish's, school's, or my own list of priorities.

Check any statements that may be true of your catechists in your situation:

____ I went to Catholic school. I know my faith.

____ I work all week and there is no time to attend catechist formation.

____ I cannot afford a babysitter in order to attend sessions.

____ I am already overextended and in my free time I want to be with my family.

____ I will sound very stupid. I did not have much training in my faith.

____ I really do not think I need to know all this content. After all, I just teach little kids.

____ The manual gives me all the information I need. I'll just follow it.

The demons of juggling roles, time, and priorities confound the best intentions. Your catechists want to be informed and competent. You want them to be the best catechists they can be. There is no easy answer to the dilemmas between your wants and reality. *Echoes of Faith* modules give you a tool you have not had before. The modules address the varied backgrounds, interest levels, and availability. The very fact that they provide you with flexibility in meeting the needs for basic level catechist formation frees you, the catechetical leader, to address the advanced formational needs of the more seasoned catechist.

Take a few minutes to consider the topics you could offer or projects you would be free to do, if* Echoes *met this basic need for catechist formation.

How shall they call on Him in whom they have not believed? And how can they believe unless they have heard of Him? And how can they hear unless there is someone to preach? And how can they preach unless they are sent? Scripture says: "How beautiful are the feet of those who announce good news!"

ROMANS 11:14–15

RECRUITING, ASSESSING, TRAINING, SUPPORTING, EVALUATING CATECHISTS

❖ RECRUITING CATECHISTS

Each parish needs to develop an effective method for recruiting catechists. This method should be utilized year round, not simply as the need for a catechist arises. Recruitment is the responsibility of the whole parish, but it always falls on the shoulders of the DRE. You should develop a recruitment team to assist in the process. In order to have an effective recruitment process, you need to ask yourself the following questions:

- Can I identify the role for which the person is asked to volunteer?

- Can I describe the responsibilities of a catechist?

- Can I describe the personal qualities needed by a catechist?

- Am I able to identify the skills needed by a catechist?

- Am I able to indicate the time this ministry would require (Planning, teaching, formation, attendance at meetings)?

- Am I able to indicate the availability of training?

Your recruitment plan should minimally consist of:

- Publicizing the need.

- Involving parish leaders in recruitment.
- Identifying prospective candidates.
- Establishing a procedure for contacting candidates.
- Meeting and interviewing candidates.
- Selecting persons to serve as catechists.

Please note: In most cases Catholic school religion teachers are not recruited primarily as catechists. Principals, however, should take care when interviewing potential teachers to discern whether the teacher has the necessary qualities and skills to serve as a religion teacher/catechist.

Gloria Reinhardt has worked in religious education for over twenty years at the parish, the school, and the diocesan level. Her positions have included Diocesan Coordinator for youth ministry for the diocese of Richmond, Virginia; Catholic high-school religion chairperson, director of religious education in numerous parishes, pastoral associate in the southwestern part of Virginia, college campus minister, and retreat director. She presently is the Associate Director of Religious Education for the diocese of Wilmington, Delaware. Ms. Reinhardt holds a Master of Theology degree with a concentration in religious studies from Boston College.

❖ ASSESSING CATECHISTS

If you believe the catechist is central to the catechetical experience, then the role of the catechist warrants great care and nurturing. The person desiring to be a catechist should first be interviewed by the DRE/CRE, designated catechetical leader or program coordinator in order to determine whether this person has the gifts to be a catechist. Once that has been established, you can formulate a realistic, achievable plan for ongoing faith formation. Ideally, an interview should take place each year of the catechist's ministry. In this way, the catechist develops a sense of ownership for the ministry and for his or her own personal growth and formation. Formation of all catechists should be an expectation because of the centrality of the

catechist's role to the life of the Church. Sharing the richness of our tradition requires specific skills, training and formation. Furthermore, the catechist expects assistance in their sacred role.

There are many ways to assess the experience, background and growth of catechists. Use of a standard format is very helpful. Here are some processes for assessment.

Assessment of a New Catechist

The assessment should be informal. Appendix A is a sample form: Appendix A, #a to #g, may be completed prior to the interview; Appendix A, #h to #j, is completed at the interview *only after* the catechist's suitability is determined.

Assessment of a Returning Catechist

This interview takes place at the beginning or the end of the year. Appendix B, #a to #f, is completed prior to the interview; Appendix B, #g to #I, is completed at the interview.

Although, the ideal model for developing a catechist's growth plan is the individual interview, with time constraints this might not be feasible. The following is a format for assessing a large number of catechists.

Assessment of a Group of Catechists

Assessing the needs and establishing a growth plan for a group of catechists:

- The format is a reflective experience.
- Use the video and companion booklet for *The Person of the Catechist* page 13.
- Catechists should have their individual companion booklet.
- For each catechist have enough *Echoes of Faith* Content Posters (available from RCL).
- The process is:
  - *Growing as a Catechist,* page 13—10 min. reflection and 10 min. sharing.
  - *Looking Ahead* and video segment, 3 to 15 min.
  - *Looking Back,* page 15—15 min. reflection and 15 min. sharing
  - Read the article on page 16 and develop a tentative growth plan for the year.
  - Share the plan with the assigned mentor.

❖ TRAINING CATECHISTS

Many people are responsible for and contribute to a religious education program in a parish and school. Catechists, especially, are key ingredients in a successful program. Catechists are a diverse group of individuals. In a typical parish program you will find:

- Those with little experience and a lot of anxiety.
- "Oldtimers" who have a sure grasp of their role but need a new wave of enthusiasm.
- Catechists with a strong theological background but lacking in practical teaching techniques.
- Some who are creative but may be weak in identifying the "Message" with clarity and precision.

Echoes of Faith helped us to see that catechist formation is the most important part of teaching in a Catholic school. The teachers could relate to the methodology and enjoyed sharing with staff members what they do in religion class. The modules are well done and help stimulate discussion.

SR. JOSEPHANN WAGONER, SSND,
PRINCIPAL
CATHOLIC COMMUNITY
ELEMENTARY/MIDDLE SCHOOL
BALTIMORE, MD

Mary Braitman has been a catechist in the Archdiocese of Los Angeles for almost thirty years. She has worked with all age groups from early childhood through adult. Ms. Braitman served as a parish director of religious education for twelve years and as a parish adult education coordinator for eight years. She has been a master catechist for sixteen years and has served on many ministry formation teams. She currently serves as regional consultant for the Archdiocese of Los Angeles Office of Religious Education, providing resources and consultation for Ventura and Santa Barbara counties. She holds a Bachelor of Arts degree in English from California State University, Northridge.

The leader of the parish or school religious education program must respond to these various needs to insure that the catechist is properly prepared to fulfill their role. A parish can choose to fulfill its responsibility for catechist formation in a variety of ways.

The key to any successful catechist formation is a good assessment of the catechist's gifts, abilities, and needs. (Refer to assessment forms in Appendix A on pages 33–34.)

One approach to catechist formation is to see it in three phases:

1. ORIENTATION—This is an opportunity to gather those interested in being catechists for the first time with those who are experienced catechists in your program. It provides time for the experienced catechists to join the DRE/principal in:
   * Explaining the importance of the catechetical ministry.
   * Identifying who are the catechists of the parish/school.
   * Explaining where this catechetical program fits into the total catechetical effort of the parish/school.
   * Explaining what the role of a catechist is.
   * Explaining how a catechist fulfills that role in this parish/school.
   * Explaining the importance of catechist formation.

2. INITIAL TRAINING—In whatever way a parish or school decides to provide initial training for catechists, it would be important to include both educational and spiritual formation based on reliable resources and catechetical guidelines. *Echoes of Faith* is a basic catechist formation program that provides both formation and information.

3. ONGOING FORMATION—Following the initial training experience, catechists should be offered periodic, planned opportunities for educational and spiritual growth.

❖ SUPPORTING CATECHISTS

During the religious education year all catechists, but especially the new catechists, need continual support and encouragement. Remind them to reread and reflect on the supplemental articles and the "Looking Beyond" sections in their *Echoes of Faith* booklets. Encourage their assigned mentor to meet periodically with the catechists to share seasonal activities and to share their thoughts and questions from the completed *Echoes of Faith* companion booklets. In addition to helping new catechists in this way, parishes and schools can support their catechists both directly and indirectly. Ongoing support is one of the most significant factors in retaining catechists.

INDIRECT SUPPORT—this involves the behind-the-scenes preparation before a catechist ever appears on the scene.

• Clear definition of expectations, including time commitment and training expectations.

• Orientation and training.

• Financial resources and resources for training, and materials.

DIRECT SUPPORT—planned efforts to meet needs of individuals and provide a sense of worth and importance.

Personal Support

• Awareness of needs.
• Sharing of information.
• Opportunity for involvement.
• Keeping records of service and training.
• Observing the catechist—the DRE or designated catechetical leader should observe the catechist during the year. The observation should be for a full session in a catechetical experience demonstrating the skills learned.

Relational Support

• Knowing catechists' names.
• Expressions of gratitude.
• Regular meetings.
• Assistance in planning.
• Occasional remembrances for holidays, birthdays, anniversaries.
• Parish recognition, such as a commissioning service.

Educational Support

• Providing resources necessary to teach.
• Providing training to utilize resources effectively.
• Ongoing formation opportunities.

Echoes of Faith has been most useful for orientation of new catechists who have little or no previous experience and training. Our professional school teachers have found the program challenging, revitalizing and renewing.

SR. NANCY STILES, DRE
SACRED HEART PARISH
GLYNDON, MD

Recruiting persons for ministry is only half the task. Without consistent and ongoing support— the hard follow through— enablement will not take place.

MUTUAL MINISTRY,
FENHAGEN, 105

❖ EVALUATING CATECHISTS

How does one know he or she is a good catechist? The answer to this question is "wrapped up" in the process of evaluation. Evaluation is one of the most important and the most neglected aspects of religious education programs. The most careful planning, the most elaborate program designs or individual classroom sessions, will be useless if evaluation does not take place to determine if goals have been met or objectives completed.

Sister. Rosalie Digenan, D.C.,
is currently the Director of
Religious Education for the
Diocese of Springfield/Cape
Girardeau, Missouri. She has
been involved in education,
special education, spiritual
direction, pastoral formation, and
religious education over the past
forty-seven years. Sr. Rosalie
holds a master's degree in
education from St. Louis
University and a bachelor's
degree from Fontbonne College
in St. Louis.

Simply stated, evaluation is the process of looking back. The catechist looks back and reviews the catechetical year. "Where am I in terms of my agreed upon goals and my personal expectations as a catechist." A catechist will respond favorably to review and evaluation, if first they are made aware of the *methods and times of evaluation* before they commit themselves to teach. Also, the evaluation process is simplified by input from the DRE/CRE, designated catechetical leader, program coordinator, or assigned mentor, but, in the end, it is the catechist who assesses himself or herself. The GDC states the three dimensions of catechist formation as being, knowing, and *savoir faire*. The yearly evaluation should address these three areas:

- How have you grown as a believer?
- How have you grown in knowledge of the message?
- What skills have you acquired which assisted you in transmitting the message?

Evaluation will be a positive experience if it results in some improvement for the existing situation or an affirmation of what is taking place. To make the evaluation a growth experience:

- Use the assessment tool page from the *Echoes of Faith* companion booklet. This assessment page (last page) has issues and questions surfaced by the catechist, which could be the starting point of the interview.
- Incorporate insights gathered from observation of the catechist's classes by the DRE/CRE, program coordinator, or the designated catechetical leader.
- Adjust Appendix B for use as an end-of-the-year evaluation tool.
- Record completion of growth experiences on Appendices D and E.

This review should act as a springboard for the discussion concerning ongoing formation. In this way, the catechist will understand how the evaluation process contributes to their personal growth and the development of the overall program.

For additional ideas on recruiting, assessing, training, supporting, and evaluating volunteer catechists, refer to "The Effective DRE: A Skills Development Series" developed by the National Conference Of Catechetical Leadership and published by Loyola Press.

WHAT IS ECHOES OF FAITH?

OVERVIEW

Echoes of Faith is a video assisted, basic catechist formation program to meet the needs of a new generation of catechists. It is a program designed by the catechetical community for the catechetical community. If you examine these two sentences more closely, you will be able to understand *Echoes* even better.

Video Assisted Learning

Echoes is much more than a video with a study guide. It is an integrated learning design with a video component. In order to gain the maximum benefit from the program, the participants must follow the learning process in the companion booklet. The process in the book drives the learning with different activities, articles and reflections developed to help the participant integrate the learning with his/her own experience.

Basic Catechist Formation

Echoes provides a solid foundation for a catechist in the three dimensions of formation suggested by the *General Directory for Catechesis* (GDC), article 238. The GDC suggests that the three dimensions of formation are: being, knowing, and *savoir faire.*

- "Being" refers to the spiritual and human formation of the catechist him/herself. The GDC points out that this formation of the catechist's own spiritual and human life is critically important. Two modules of the project, *The Person of the Catechist* and *The Roles of the Catechist,* focus on the catechist's own self-understanding and maturation. Each of these modules will take a minimum of two hours to complete.

- Five modules focus on "knowing." The GDC emphasizes the

As with any other art the most important factor is that the catechist should acquire [his/her] own style of imparting catechesis by adapting the general principles of catechetical pedagogy to [his/her] own personality.

GENERAL DIRECTORY FOR CATECHESIS (GDC), 244

importance of the catechist having a "sufficient knowledge of the message." It also reminds us that the *Catechism of the Catholic Church* is the fundamental doctrinal reference point. The five theological modules of *Echoes* are rooted in the *Catechism*. Four of them; *The Creed, Liturgy and Sacraments, Morality,* and *Prayer and Spirituality* are related to the four main sections of the *Catechism*. The fifth one focuses on *Scripture* which is the "soul of all theological study." Each of these modules will take at least four hours to complete.

- The GDC introduces an interesting word into the catechetical vocabulary, *savoir faire,* as the third area of formation. It is the ability to communicate the Gospel message. *Echoes* helps the catechist gain this *savoir faire* by offering modules on *Getting Started as a Catechist, Methodology for Grades 1–2, 3–4, 5–6, 7–8* and a final module on *The Learner. Getting Started* and *Methods* are each two-hour modules. *The Learner* takes a minimum of four hours to complete.

Echoes provides a minimum of thirty hours of formation covering the three areas of formation suggested in the GDC. However, it is not comprehensive

nor is it sufficient for the fully formed catechist. It is basic. It introduces the catechist to ideas, concepts they will encounter as they progress in their formation as catechists.

The Needs of a New Generation of Catechists

As we have seen, the new generation of catechists bring some special gifts to the ministry, as well as some special needs. They are a generation on the go, leading very busy lives, working outside of the home. *Echoes* provides the director of religious education and/or principal with a tool to meet their need for *flexibility* as to when the catechist can engage in formation.

Each module is self-contained. It does not depend on any other module. It can be done in a large group, a small group, or individually. Such *flexibility* is essential if the question is, "How can I assist this catechist in getting adequate formation to be effective and competent?" not "How can I get the catechist to a certain location at a certain time on a certain day in order to . . . ?" *Echoes* allows the director to literally tailor the formation program to fit the life schedule of the catechist!

The new generation is also very *visual*. They learn best in a multi-sensory environment. *Echoes* provides high-quality video production which engages and captures the attention of the participants. The videos include many location shots featuring real catechists in real situations. The catechists can see how others work with children, youth, and adults in diverse catechetical settings. The videos also convey content through story and the life experiences of actual people.

Finally, the new generation of catechists comes lacking a solid foundation in the vocabulary of the faith. The theological modules attempt to present a clear exposition of the basic concepts and words which comprise the heart of the Catholic Christian Tradition in an appealing way.

These are just a few of the ways *Echoes of Faith* attempts to meet the needs of the persons who will be your catechists as you move into the new mil lennium.

Echoes was designed by the catechetical community for the catechetical community.

By the Catechetical Community

The National Conference of Catechetical Leadership (NCCL) is the only national association dedicated solely to catechesis. Its members come from diocesan offices, parish DREs, academics who focus on catechesis, and the publishing community. It is truly a collaborative project involving some of the very best talents in the catechetical community.

Resources for Christian Living (RCL) provided the funding and the expertise to bring the dream of NCCL to life. Over a period of three years they committed staff and finances to *Echoes*. Oblate Media Communications Corporation (OMCC), a leading light in Catholic video production, provided the video production.

Principle content specialists and consultants include:

Ms. Janaan Mantarnach and Mr. Carl Pfeiffer—*Getting Started as a Catechist*

Sr. Ann Marie Mongoven and Rev. Michael Moynahan—*The Roles of the Catechist*

Mr. Thomas Groome—*The Person of the Catechist*

Fr. Donald Senior—*I Believe, We Believe* (The Creed)

Sr. Catherine Dooley—*Liturgy and Sacraments*

Fr. Richard Sparks—*Morality*

Bishop Robert Morneau—*Prayer and Spirituality*

Sr. Mary Boys—*Scripture*

Ms. Irene Murphy—*Methodology for Grades 1–2, 3–4, 5–6, 7–8*

Ms. Evelyn and Mr. James Whitehead—*The Learner*

We are becoming community! We're in this together! Through Echoes of Faith, we get to know each other and share with one another. I've taught CCD before. I came, did my hour, left and never spoke to anyone except the children I taught. But now I hear what others think. We talk about important things of the heart, the Church, what we believe! It helps us all grow and become better catechists.

TERESA LEICHT, CATECHIST
HOLY CROSS PARISH
CUBA, MO

Echoes brings you learning modules shaped by these experts and filled out with articles and other contributions from more than seventy-five nationally known educators, catechists, liturgists, and theologians. You now have the very best of the catechetical community's expertise right in your parish.

Since it is a project with a national reach, an advisory board of bishops and staff from other national associations and organizations, e.g. USCC and NCEA, helped to guide the project in its formative stages. NCCL has made every effort to ensure that your catechists are getting the very best formation available.

For the Catechetical Community
Echoes is designed to be very practical and adaptable. In Part III you will see several ways to implement *Echoes*. Parish DREs played a vital role in helping to shape the modules, in their content and style. Diocesan directors of religious education gave valuable input to ensure that the *Echoes* modules would fit into most diocesan formation/certification programs. In short, every effort was made to make *Echoes* the most user friendly catechist formation program available.

CORE CONTENT OF MODULES

❖THEOLOGICAL MODULES

I Believe/We Believe
- God, the Creator of all that exists.
- God's revelation in human history.
- The call to relationship that God offers to each human being.
- Faith as a response to God's call.
- Scripture and Sacred Tradition as the primary modes of God's revelation.
- Jesus Christ as the fullness of God's revelation.
- God as Trinity of persons.
- The Incarnation.
- The Holy Spirit as animator of the community of faith.
- The Church as the Body of Christ, the community of believers.
- Creeds as summary statements of the community about its core beliefs.
- The Nicene Creed.

VIDEO TIMES

❖ I BELIEVE / WE BELIEVE
Segment 1:	Part A:	13 min.
	Part B:	10 min.
Segment 2:	Part A:	9 min.
	Part B:	13 min.
Segment 3:	Part A:	9 min.
	Part B:	12 min.
Segment 4:	Part A:	12 min.
	Part B:	7 min.

❖ LITURGY AND SACRAMENTS
Segment 1:	21 min
Segment 2:	19 min.
Segment 3:	19 min.
Segment 4:	14 min.

Liturgy and Sacraments

- The meaning of ritual.
- The nature of liturgy.
- The relationship of liturgy to the Paschal mystery.
- The celebration of liturgy in a cycle of time.
- The role of space, music, and cultural expression in liturgy.
- The importance of the assembly in liturgical celebration.
- The way in which symbolic actions express meaning and invite participation in the saving action they celebrate.
- The sacramental principle.
- The relationship of the seven sacraments to the fundamental experiences of human life.
- The centrality of Eucharist in the Church.
- Baptism, Confirmation, and Eucharist as the sacraments of initiation.
- Penance and Reconciliation and the Anointing of the Sick as the two sacraments that celebrate healing.
- The sacraments of Holy Orders and Matrimony as celebrating the two central vocations at the service of communion.

Catholic Morality

- Human dignity and community as the foundations of the moral life.
- The meaning of virtue and its foundations in the teachings of Jesus.
- The implications of the Beatitudes for daily life.
- The meaning and validity of objective morality.
- The sources for arriving at objective moral truth.
- The delicate relationship between objective moral truth and subjective, or personal, responsibility.
- Moral actions as the responses one makes to the grace offered by a loving God.
- Moral actions as a combination of act, intention, and circumstance.
- The nature, origin, and degrees of sin.
- The effects of sin on the individual and the community.
- The nature of conscience and the process of informing one's conscience.
- The timeless quality and universal validity of the Commandments.
- The relationship of the Commandments to the new law of Jesus Christ.

Prayer and Spirituality

- The basic dynamic of prayer as listening and responding to God's call.
- The Angelus as an example of the dynamic of prayer.
- Mary as the perfect model of acceptance and response to God's call.

The Liturgy and Sacraments module gave me a new appreciation and a different perspective on sacramental life.

MARILYN SCROOPE MAHONEY
ST. BERNADETTE PARISH
SEVERN, MD

VIDEO TIMES

❖ CATHOLIC MORALITY
Segment 1: Part A: 8 min.
Part B: 9 min.
Segment 2: Part A: 9 min.
Part B: 10 min.
Segment 3: Part A: 9 min.
Part B: 8 min.
Segment 4: Part A: 10 min.
Part B: 10 min.

❖ PRAYER AND SPIRITUALITY
Segment 1: 7 min
Segment 2: 15 min.
Segment 3: 12 min.
Segment 4: 15 min.

- The relationship between personal prayer and the community of faith.
- The various prayer forms through which we make our response to God.
- Obstacles to the life of prayer.
- The Holy Spirit as source of our prayer response.
- Prayer, service, and asceticism as the three foundations of the spiritual life.
- The Our Father as the bedrock of Christian prayer.

Introduction to the Scriptures
- The Bible as the Word of God.
- The formation of the Scriptures over time.
- The importance of context in reading the Bible.
- Some literary forms found in the Bible.
- The meaning of inspiration.
- The establishment of the canon of the Scriptures.
- The biblical themes of covenant and freedom.
- The source of the Bible's holiness.
- The root story of the Exodus.
- The relationship of Jesus' saving action to the Exodus event.
- The basic message of Jesus in the gospels.
- The role of Paul in spreading the good news of Jesus Christ.

❖ CATECHETICAL MODULES

Getting Started as a Catechist
- Creating the physical environment for catechesis.
- Shaping a social environment in which faith can be nurtured.
- Using creative activities in learning.
- Developing successful session plans.
- Managing positive behavior in the catechetical setting.
- Helping learners pray together.

Roles of the Catechist
- Storytelling in religious education.
- The quality of the catechist as teacher/companion.
- The importance of leading prayer in the catechetical setting.
- The role of the catechist as a witness for justice.

The Person of the Catechist
- The vocation of the catechist.
- The role of the catechist in the Church's ministry.
- The qualities of a catechist as expressed in contemporary Church documents.

- The importance of the catechist's continued growth and understanding of the catechetical ministry.

- The role of the Spirit in the catechetical ministry of the Church.

❖ METHODOLOGICAL MODULES

Methods for Each Grade Level (Grade 1–2; 3–4; 5–6; 7–8)
- Human development characteristics.
- Developmental faith needs.
- Strategies for introducing the Scriptures and Sacred Tradition.
- The relevance of activities to faith development.
- Appropriate prayer forms.
- Inclusion of children with special needs.

Introduction to the Learner
- The nature of learning.
- The relationship of religion and science.

- Principles of developmental theory.
- The process of human knowing.
- The psycho-social development of the human person.
- Moral decision making.
- The role of imagination in moral decision making.
- The relationship between moral decisions and moral actions.
- The relationship of human knowing, relating, and acting to religious faith.
- Faith-development theory.
- The journey of faith through the seasons of childhood, discipleship, and stewardship.

FORMAT AND FLOW OF THE LEARNING PROCESS

Echoes of Faith, Phase I, has thirteen modules. Each module takes a minimum of either two or four hours to complete. The learning process for each module is contained in the companion booklet.

There is a uniform format throughout the series:

Overview
Each module begins with an overview of the entire module. It tells the participant what they should expect and some of the learnings they will achieve if they complete the module. Finally, the Overview encourages the participant to have a companion as they

VIDEO TIMES

❖ METHODS GRADES 1 AND 2
Segment 1: 12 min.
Segment 2: 12 min.
Segment 3: 10 min.
Segment 4: no video

❖ METHODS GRADES 3 AND 4
Segment 1: 12 min
Segment 2: 10 min.
Segment 3: 13 min.
Segment 4: no video

❖ METHODS GRADES 5 AND 6
Segment 1: 11 min
Segment 2: 13 min.
Segment 3: 12 min.
Segment 4: no video

❖ METHODS GRADES 7 AND 8
Segment 1: 11 min
Segment 2: 13 min.
Segment 3: 12 min.
Segment 4: no video

❖ INTRODUCTION TO THE LEARNER
Before You Begin: 10 min
Segment 1: 7 min.
Segment 2: 7 min.
Segment 3: 10 min.
Segment 4: no video

> *Echoes of Faith is a combination of solid content, beautiful images and touching stories all tied together to present a theme. Each module allows the participant to renew his/her own faith while sharing experiences with other teachings and building confidence for the task of teaching.*
>
> RITA C. HUTZELL, TEACHER
> ST. MARY PARISH SCHOOL
> HAGERSTOWN, MARYLAND

move through the process. This companion may be the DRE or a master catechist. It may even be someone on the diocesan staff who can answer any questions or concerns which may emerge from the process.

There are some catechetical leaders who are uncomfortable with a catechist moving through the module on her/his own, without being part of a group. This concern often comes from the deeply held belief that our faith is not a private faith, but a shared faith. The insight about our faith being a communal faith is a true one. However, it does not mean that a catechist or believer cannot ever learn on his/her own. *Echoes* allows a catechist to complete a module on his/her own schedule. *Echoes* also assumes that at the completion of the module there will be a gathering or a meeting at which time, learnings can be confirmed, shared, etc.

Opening Prayer
Each module provides a prayer to begin the session.

Before You Begin
The first movement in the learning is to help the catechist focus on the topic at hand. It attempts to get the catechist in touch with his/her own experience which relates to the topic.

Segments
Each module is broken down into a series of segments (usually four per module). Each segment has several movements as well as a video component. There are two types of videos:

- Methodology videos are documentary style featuring catechist interviews, demonstrations by catechists, and summary graphics.
- Theology videos use rich visuals and stories to illustrate content. The approach is holistic, focusing on the cognitive, behavioral, and affective senses of the viewer.

Introduction and Learning Objectives
Each segment begins by presenting the participant with a list of the learning objectives for the section. It helps the learner identify what they already know and challenges them to think more deeply about the topic

Looking Ahead
The purpose of this section is to prepare the learner to view the video. "Watch for . . ." "Look out for . . ." alerts the participant to pay attention to certain segments in each video. Throughout the video and at the end of each segment there is a summation screen capsulizing the important points covered. The best learning theory regarding instructional

video stresses the importance of this setup. The booklet also provides a space for the viewer to write down notes.

Looking Back

After viewing the video, the learner is referred back to the booklet, to the "Looking Back" section. Here the viewer is invited to reflect on what they have seen, to react to certain statements, etc. Once again, learning theory calls for this activity as an essential element in the learning process.

Looking Beyond

One of the critical steps in learning is the ability to apply what has been learned to a new or different situation. "Looking Ahead" challenges the learner to take the skills, knowledge, etc., and apply it to a situation close to their actual catechetical situation.

Articles

The booklets also provide a number of succinct articles covering topics of special interest for further exploration. The length of the articles (no more than two pages) invites the reader to stop and take time to deepen their knowledge. The articles have been prepared with the new catechist in mind. Experts from the catechetical, theological, litur-gical, pastoral, and educational community have contributed these valuable resources.

Closing Prayer

A short prayer service is provided to conclude the module

Bibliography

There is a short bibliography at the end of each booklet to suggest further reading for the catechist.

Assessment Tool

There is an assessment tool at the end of each booklet. This page can be torn from the booklet and kept in the catechist's file as a record of the modules they have completed.

Sidebars / Boxes / Factoids

The booklets have been designed with the modern, nonlinear learner in mind. They contain important quotes, references, and, sometimes, summations of material. Don't overlook their potential!

A Program That Looks Like Our Church

The videos, the activities, and the suggestions reflect the many faces of the Roman Catholic Church in North America. Videos were shot in urban, suburban, and rural parishes. Activities are designed for adaptation in multi-cultural settings.

The Echoes of Faith related well to the lived experience of our catechists. The catechists appreciated the use of the adult learning model as a means to challenge them in their own faith experience.

SR. GEOGETTE CUNNIFF, OSF, DRE
OUR LADY OF LOURDES
PORT WENTWORTH, GEORGIA

USING *ECHOES OF FAITH*

OVERVIEW

The catechist is an educator who facilitates maturation of the faith which catechumens and those being catechized obtain with the help of the Holy Spirit.

GENERAL DIRECTORY FOR CATECHESIS (GDC), 244

Echoes of Faith has the flexibility to allow catechists to learn individually or in groups, or in a combination of group and individual work at parish, school, and regional centers. There is no one preferred method of using *Echoes*. Whatever meets the needs of the catechists and the catechetical leadership is the best way for you to use the program.

Echoes' format allows catechists maximum flexibility, suited to the demands of daily life. After assessing the catechist's individual needs, a director and the catechist determine what model is conducive to the catechist's lifestyle. (Refer to appendix A and B, side two). No matter which format is used, the Director should emphasize that the booklets are *essential* to the learning process.

The Companion booklets:
- offer articles by catechetical specialists,
- opportunities to respond and process the video content,
- provide for reflection and discussion,
- supply a wealth of tips, check lists, and practical suggestions for sharing faith,
- and applies what has been learned.

Primarily, *Echoes* is designed as a basic level of catechist formation for the beginner catechist.

THE OPTIONS FOR USE:

In Homes
- As self directed.
- As a small group of catechists or teachers who live in the same neighborhood with a designated facilitator.
- A group of catechists who find a mutually convenient time to meet.

Parish/School

- As an entire group, at a regularly scheduled catechist or teacher meeting.
- As a group gathered specifically for formation.
- As a gathering of grade level catechists or teachers.
- As a gathering of those with the same level of experience.
- As a joint formation opportunity of catechists and Catholic school teachers.
- In certain circumstances, with a single catechist and director.

In addition, it may be used as:

- Ongoing enrichment to challenge the seasoned catechists to rethink and renew their faith, teaching skills, and commitment to the ministry.
- Faith formation for RCIA catechetical team members.
- Faith and catechetical formation of the catechetical team members for RCIA adapted for children.
- Faith formation for children's liturgy of the Word.
- Parent orientation meetings.
- A retreat experience for catechists.
- Adult education groups.
- Training of home school parents.

—◆—

USES OF ECHOES OF FAITH:

1. Self-directed Model—For Use With a Mentor

Explain the following for at-home use:

- Allow sufficient time (30–45 minutes for the theological catechetical modules and one hour for theological modules) for each individual segment.
- Instruct the catechist to follow the format presented on pages 21–23 or copy it for them.
- After finishing all the segments the catechist meets with the DRE/CRE, designated catechetical leader, program coordinator, or the catechist's mentor to review the learning.

- The self-assessment tool (last page of every module booklet) is returned to the DRE/CRE or catechetical leader for recognition of accomplishment.

- An individual record of each catechist's accomplishment should be kept. (See Appendices C and D on pages 37 and 38.)

Please note: A catechist could complete the video segment and booklet individually and then participate in a subsequent group gathering for sharing and prayer.

—◆—

The video presentation accompanied by the workbook enables our busy catechists to meet in small groups most convenient to their schedules. This allows the catechists the opportunity to gain knowledge from the experts and seasoned catechists appearing in Echoes of Faith.

DEBBIE L. WILLIAMSON, DRE
ST. ANNE PARISH
BEAUMONT, TX

—◆—

Go into all the world; and preach the Gospel to the whole creation.

MARK 16:15

2. **Small Group Model—Or sharing *Echoes of Faith* in a home, parish or school setting with a designated facilitator**

Pre-planning
- Decide the number of segments to be accomplished in each meeting.
- Allow at least 45 minutes for the catechetical modules and 90 minutes for the theological modules.
- Arrange for VCR/TV and the video to be used.
- Obtain sufficient number of companion booklets.
- Pencils/Pens.
- Arrange for seating with small groups in mind.
- Designate a facilitator. (Facilitator should preview the video).
- Ask one or two people to help set up and serve simple refreshments.
- Set up a Prayer center with a Bible and candle.

Meeting Time
- Start by gathering in prayer. Use the opening prayer in the companion booklet.
- Follow the companion booklet as a guide to the format of the meeting.

- Allow for sufficient time for reflection and sharing of the companion booklet questions.
- Elicit the participants' reactions to *Echoes*. Answer any questions.
- If the group is only completing one segment at a time, conduct an informal evaluation after the segment session.

Example:
One thing I learned from the session today . . .
One thing that was challenging . . .
One thing that will help in my role as a catechist is . . .
One thing I learned from the process that I can adapt to my particular situation, learners, and grade level . . .

- Conclude with the closing prayer found in the companion booklet.
- Finish the session with some form of fellowship.
- At the last session, have the catechists fill out the self-assessment tool. Return to the DRE/CRE or designated catechetical leader.

3. **Large Group Model—For gathering in a large group at the parish**

Pre Planning
- Reserve video and order companion booklets.
- Reserve meeting room.
- Arrange for tables and chairs.

- Arrange for TV & VCR or video projector and screen.
- If group is large, enlist others to act as small group facilitators for the purpose of keeping the

process moving at individual tables.

- Ask one or two people to help purchase and serve refreshments.
- Gather material for prayer table.
- Preview video and booklet and decide how many segments of the module you will use each night.
- Decide on the time for each activity.
- Publicize with catechists/teachers.
- Divide catechists attending into small groups of three to five.
- Arrange for help setting up the room.
- Prepare check-in sheets, name tags, and group numbers.

Meeting Time

- Welcome participants.
- Provide name tags and group assignments. Give each participant a companion booklet.
- Start with a gathering prayer (See companion booklet for a suggested prayer).
- Review guidelines for sharing in a group (see below).
- Use the companion booklet as a guide for the format of the session (see pages 21–23 for format).
- It is not necessary to use all the questions in each segment. Use one or two questions in each segment and direct the participants to complete the others on their own.
- Allow for sufficient time for personal reflection and sharing in small groups.
- Conduct a brief evaluation. Some possible questions may be:
  —What did I learn?
  —What was one thing that was challenging?
  —What did I learn that could be used in my classroom or catechetical setting?
  —What was one thing I learned that will make me a more effective catechist/teacher?
  —What is one thing that would have made this a more effective learning experience for me?
- Conclude with a prayer. (See companion booklet for suggestions.)
- Allow time for fellowship and refreshments.

We are just beginning to use Echoes of Faith and are excited about the flexibility and sensitivity this program offers to the catechist. With the busy schedules of today, the video/workbooks make it possible for the catechist to learn at his/her own pace.

SHEILA MEARA, DRE
ST. MARY MAGDALEN
WILMINGTON, DE

GUIDELINES FOR GROUP SHARING:

1. Share your self and your experiences. They are important and may be a source of significant learning or insight for another member of the group. Use "I" statements rather than "they" statements.

2. Listen closely to others in the group. They have much to share and you may learn a

great deal from their experiences and ideas.

3. Show support for others in the group without giving advice, criticizing, or confronting. Everyone is gathered because they want to learn. Honor each person's commitment to the ministry.

4 Respectfully correct any misinformation that may be given by a member of the group.

5. Encourage everyone to share. Each person's insights, opinions, and ideas are valuable.

6. Do not dominate the discussion.

7. Stay on the topic being discussed. Should the conversation stray, gently bring it back to the original topic.

8. Respect the confidentiality of the group.

OTHER APPLICATIONS

1. Using *Echoes of Faith* in Catholic Schools

Echoes of Faith is being utilized in Catholic Schools all across the United States. Principals are finding it an effective tool for forming Catholic school teachers who teach religion.

Options for Gathering the Faculty

If the entire faculty teaches religion you can gather them:

- During a portion of an in-service day.

- For an hour after school (you can complete one or two segments of a module in an hour).

- In small groups at a time convenient to them.

- Individually in their home and then gather as a large group to reflect on people's insights and questions.

If only a portion of the faculty teaches religion or only a small group needs basic formation you can gather them:

- During a portion of a faculty meeting or in-service while other staff are meeting on other topics.

- An hour before or after school each week.

- In a teacher's home.

- Combine an after-school meeting with a pot luck dinner.

- Work individually with the video and booklet at home and then gather to share insights and questions.

If only one or two teachers need basic catechist formation:

- Invite them to work with the booklet and video at home and then meet with the principal, religion chairperson, catechetical leaders, or experienced religion teacher to share insights and questions.

Helpful Hints

Assess the needs of your faculty in the area of catechist formation. This is particularly appropriate at the end of the year teacher review. This is an excellent time to assess needs and set goals for the new year.

The process is only effective when the video and companion booklets are used together.

The *Getting Started* module was designed for volunteer catechists and may not be appropriate for Catholic school teachers.

The theology modules are excellent for use with the entire faculty. They are helpful not only for the religion teachers but are also helpful in assisting non-Catholic teachers in understanding what we believe.

See the section on Uses of *Echoes of Faith* (page 25) for helpful ideas in planning sessions. Consider working with your parish catechetical leader to plan joint formation opportunities.

To ensure the working of the catechetical ministry in a local Church, it is fundamental to have adequate pastoral care of catechists.

Besides being a witness, the catechist must also be a teacher who teaches the faith.

GENERAL DIRECTORY FOR CATECHESIS (GDC), 233, 240

2. **Using *Echoes of Faith* for a Catechist Retreat—
(Use *The Person of the Catechist* Module, Segment 1 and 2)**
(This retreat should take place before the beginning of the religious education program or in early fall. Segment 3 may be used for assessment and Segment 4 for an evening reflection midway in the year.)

Pre-Planning

- Choose a comfortable setting either at the parish, retreat center, or home. (Please note: getting away from the familiar is important for a retreat experience. This is preferred for daylong retreats but essential for overnight experiences.)

- Arrange for sufficient refreshments.

- Name tags—if catechists do not know each other.

- Pencils/pens.

- Provide sufficient companion booklets, *The Person of the Catechist.*

- Set up a prayer center with a Bible, candle, and a large bowl of water.

- Plan the use of symbols. (Symbols can be incorporated into the prayer in many ways. Example: use of a piece of tapestry or course fabric because the article by Dr. Eipers states: "As catechists, we are weavers of the tapestry of faith."

- If the DRE/CRE or designated catechetical leader is not conducting the retreat, designate a leader and facilitators.

- Arrange for VCR/TV and the video *The Person of the Catechist.*

Using *Echoes of Faith* ·········· **29** ··········

Go into all the world; and preach the Gospel to the whole creation.

MARK 16:15

It is so affirming and enriching, helping teachers realize, yes, I can do this!

SR. EILEEN FRIEL, DRE
HOLY ROSARY PARISH
MONROE CITY

Day Schedule *(Length of time is determined by group size—Remember not to rush any section.)*

9:00 Welcome/Gathering—provide light refreshments Possible incorporation of an icebreaker (i.e., creating nametags by incorporating their names with gifts and talents like a crossword).

9:30 Opening Prayer—create a prayer service incorporating the opening prayer on page vii of *The Person of the Catechist*.

10:00 Overview of the day
  a. Develop from page vi. It is important for the catechists to realize during this day that they will explore the vocation of the catechist and the qualities of the catechist.
  b. Solicit from the catechists their expectations for this time together.

10:15 *The Vocation of the Catechist* (page 1)—Leader gives short input and then allows time for sharing *Your Thoughts*.

10:45 Quiet time—Read and reflect quietly on the article by Bishop Banks and answer the question on page viii.

11:00 Break

11:15 Brainstorm from the large group some of the answers to the reflection question on page viii. Lead into *Looking Ahead* on page 2. Show segment one.

11:45 *Looking Back* reflection and sharing

12:15 Lunch

1:00 Regather. Read the article on page 4. Large group sharing of the insights gained.

1:30 Introduction to *The Qualities of the Catechist* (page 7).

2:00 *Looking Ahead* and video segment 2 (page 8).

2:30 *Looking Back* (page 9) 15 min. for reflection—15 min. sharing in small groups.

3:00 Quiet time—complete *Called To Proclaim* (page 10) and reflection questions on page 11.

3:30 Large group sharing

4:00 Closing Eucharistic Liturgy or Prayer Service.

Evening Schedule *(midpoint in the year)*

Pre-Planning
(same items as day retreat)
Schedule (2–3 hours)
• Opening Prayer (page vii) (15 min.)—Use the piece of tapestry as part of the prayer center.
• Reflection and Sharing—Boxed area on page 18 (30 min.).
• *Trusting the Spirit* (page 19)—Give small input and allow for reflection time and sharing (30 min.).

- *Looking Ahead* and Video on page 20—(15 min.)

- *Looking Back* on page 21— (15 min. reflection and 15 min. sharing).

- Quiet time—Read the article *Trust the Spirit Within* and complete the reflection question on page 23. Allow for large group sharing or, if the group is large, groups of four.

- *Looking Beyond* on page 24— Instruct the catechists to create a small group response. Share with large group (30 min.).

- Closing Prayer—Formulate from page 27.

- Finish the session with some form of fellowship.

3. Using *Echoes of Faith* to Train RCIA Catechist Teams

Over a yearlong process, the team should use the following theology videos with the companion booklets, to enhance their background. The readings and reflective questions are useful for team sharing. The booklets will become a resource library. Follow the format reference in small group sharing on page 25.

Theological Modules
(Five four-hour modules)
    I Believe, We Believe
      (The Profession of Faith)
    Liturgy and Sacraments
    Catholic Morality
    Prayer and Spirituality
    Introduction to the Scriptures.

Also RCL • Resources for Christian Living has correlated the series *Foundations in Faith* with *Echoes of Faith. Foundations In Faith* is a complete resource library for your parish RCIA process. The correlation with the use of the *Echoes'* theological modules offers a comprehensive plan of formation. (Check out RCL catalogue.)

Echoes of Faith is an excellent resource to invite the catechists to share their faith and so reap the joy of their learners expressing their faith.

SR. MADELEINE DE WITT, DRE
ST. GEORGE PARISH
LINN, MO

4. Using *Echoes of Faith* to Train Catechist Teams for Children's Initiation and for Children's Liturgy of the Word.

The methodology videos feature catechist interviews, demonstrations by catechists, and feature articles by specialists. The following would be beneficial in assisting the teams in developing age-appropriate strategies as well as theological background. The *Introduction to the Scriptures* would prove beneficial to the Children's Liturgy of the Word teams. For use, follow the format on pages 21–23.

THEOLOGICAL MODULES	CATECHETICAL MODULES
I believe, We believe	Getting Started as a Catechist
Liturgy and Sacraments	The Person of the Catechist
Catholic Morality	Roles of the Catechist
Prayer and Spirituality	Introduction to the Learner
Introduction to the Scriptures	Methods for Grades 1 and 2
	Methods for Grades 3 and 4
	Methods for Grades 5 and 6
	Methods for Grades 7 and 8

5. Using *Echoes of Faith* for the Initial Parent Meeting

The introductory segments of the methodology modules, in which the process of intellectual and spiritual development is explained, would be beneficial to parents at the first parent meeting of the year. It would provide them with greater insight into the philosophy and approach of catechetical materials used in the parish programs. Additionally, it would assist parents in understanding more fully their role as models of faith and the primary teachers of their children. Use the large group format on page 26. Some parents might be interested in the self-directed model. Have some booklets available.

6. Using *Echoes of Faith* for Adult Education Session

All the theology modules are beneficial for small faith sharing communities. The companion booklet would serve as a journal for reflection and discussion in the small groups. Follow the format for the small group on page 25.

7. Using *Echoes of Faith* for Home Schooling

Some parents opt to teach their children at home. No matter how well-intentioned their motives, there is a need of formation. These parents could follow the self-directed model on page 25.

APPENDIX A
New Catechist Interview

Name _____   Daytime Phone_____

Address _____   Evening Phone _____

E-Mail Address_____

A. Past Experience as a catechist

B. Formal Religious Education Background

      Elementary _____(years)   College _____ (credits)

      High School _____(years)   Adult education _____

C. Why are you interested in being a catechist?

D. What in your background will assist you in being a catechist?

E. What gifts/talents do you bring to the teaching ministry?

F. What practical concern(s) do you have about teaching and sharing your faith?

G. How do you hope to grow through your teaching ministry?

H. Given your background and having reviewed the *Echoes* content poster, which *Echoes of Faith* modules will you complete in order to improve your ability as a catechist and grow as an adult believer this year? (A person who has NEVER been a catechist should begin by completing the "Getting Started" module, then complete the "Roles of the Catechist and The Person of the Catechist" modules.)

Check the appropriate modules:

THEOLOGICAL MODULES
__I Believe, We Believe
__Liturgy and Sacraments
__Catholic Morality
__Prayer and Spirituality
__Introduction to the Scriptures

CATECHETICAL MODULES
__Getting Started as a Catechist
__The Person of a Catechist
__Roles of the Catechist
__Introduction to the Learner
__Methods for Grades 1 and 2 or
__Methods for Grades 3 and 4 or
__Methods for Grades 5 and 6 or
__Methods for Grades 7 and 8

I. Given your schedule which format of *Echoes of Faith* modules would be more conducive.

__Self-directed with a mentor.

__Small group (in a home setting) with a designated facilitator.

__Gathering in a group at a parish with a designated leader.

J. Given your schedule, what times are convenient. *(Please check ALL appropriate items)*

Monday	Tuesday	Wednesday	Thursday	Friday	Saturday	Sunday
__*Morning*	__*Morning*	__*Morning*	__*Morning*	__*Morning*	__*Morning*	__*Morning*
__*Afternoon*	__*Afternoon*	__*Afternoon*	__*Afternoon*	__*Afternoon*	__*Afternoon*	__*Afternoon*
__*Evening*	__*Evening*	__*Evening*	__*Evening*	__*Evening*	__*Evening*	__*Evening*

I commit myself to continuing growth by completing _____ *Echoes of Faith* modules.

Signature of the Catechist _____

Signature of the Interviewer _____

Date _____

Assigned Mentor _____

Appendix B
Returning Catechist Annual Interview

Name _____ E-Mail _____

Years experienced as Catechist _____ Grade taught last year _____

A. Since you were interviewed last year, what happened in your experience as a catechist to keep you returning to this ministry?

B. What may have discouraged you?

C. Looking back at this year as a catechist, what did you learn about your abilities as a catechist?

D. What did you learn about yourself as an adult Catholic?

E. During the previous interview, you committed yourself to continuing growth through the completion of a specific *Echoes of Faith* module. What questions or issues arose from the completion of the module?

F. How was the learning module helpful in your service as a catechist?

G. What *Echoes of Faith* modules and growth opportunities will you participate in to improve your ability as a catechist and grow as an adult believer next/this year?

THEOLOGICAL MODULES
__I Believe, We Believe
__Liturgy and Sacraments
__Catholic Morality
__Prayer and Spirituality
__Introduction to the Scriptures

CATECHETICAL MODULES
__Getting Started as a Catechist
__The Person of a Catechist
__Roles of the Catechist
__Introduction to the Learner
__Methods for Grades 1 and 2 or
__Methods for Grades 3 and 4 or
__Methods for Grades 5 and 6 or
__Methods for Grades 7 and 8

H. Given your schedule, which format of *Echoes of Faith* modules would be more conducive.

__Self-directed with a mentor.

__Small group (in a home setting) with a designated facilitator.

__Gathering in a group at a parish with a designated leader.

I. Given your schedule, what times are convenient. *(Please check ALL appropriate items)*

Monday	Tuesday	Wednesday	Thursday	Friday	Saturday	Sunday
__*Morning*	__*Morning*	__*Morning*	__*Morning*	__*Morning*	__*Morning*	__*Morning*
__*Afternoon*	__*Afternoon*	__*Afternoon*	__*Afternoon*	__*Afternoon*	__*Afternoon*	__*Afternoon*
__*Evening*	__*Evening*	__*Evening*	__*Evening*	__*Evening*	__*Evening*	__*Evening*

I commit myself to continuing growth in_____*Echoes of Faith* modules.

Signature of Catechist _____

Signature of Interviewer _____

Assigned Mentor _____

Date _____

APPENDIX C
End of the Year Interview

Name _____ Grade taught _____

Completed *Echoes of Faith* modules _____

1. Looking back at this year as a catechist, what did you learn about your abilities as a catechist? What did you learn about yourself as an adult Catholic?

2. During the previous interview, you committed yourself to continuing growth through the completion of a specific *Echoes of Faith* module. What questions or issues arose from the completion of the module? How was the learning module helpful in your service as a catechist?

3. What *Echoes of Faith* learning module will you participate in to improve your ability as a catechist and grow as an adult believer in the coming year?

I commit myself to continuing growth by completing _____ *Echoes of Faith* learning modules.

Signature of the Catechist _____

Signature of the Interviewer _____

Assigned Mentor _____

Date _____

Record of Catechist Formation

Catechist's name _____

	Date	Topic of Formation	Instructor or Facilitator	Place	Hours	Method Use (Echoes or another form of formation, such as attendance at a Diocesan certification program)	Mentor/ Companion's Name
1.							
2.							
3.							
4.							
5.							
6.							
7.							
8.							
9.							
10.							
11.							
12.							
13.							
14.							
15.							

Comments: _____

(Use multiple forms for more than 10 persons.)

APPENDIX E

Echoes of Faith Record of Use
(Place Date of Completion)

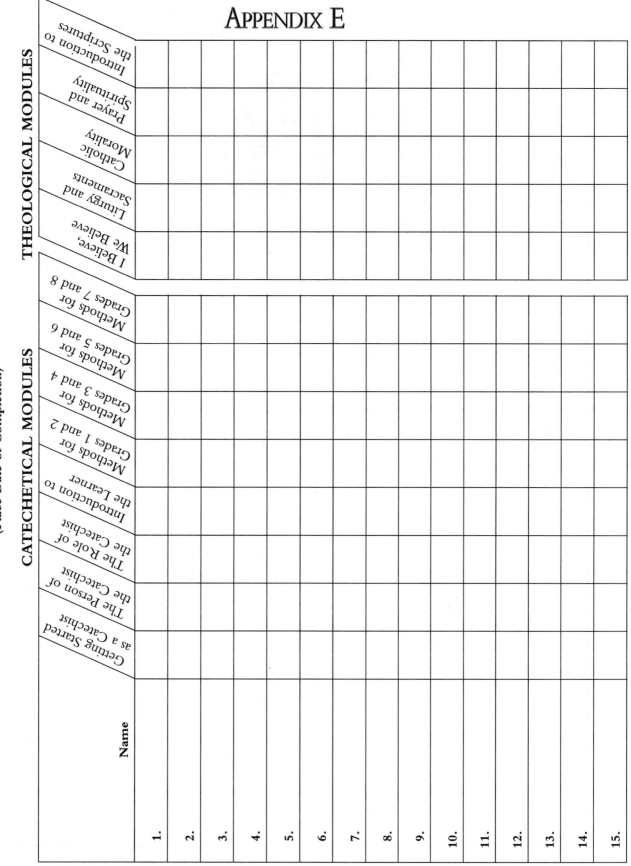

THEOLOGICAL MODULES

- Introduction to the Scriptures
- Prayer and Spirituality
- Catholic Morality
- Liturgy and Sacraments
- I Believe, We Believe

CATECHETICAL MODULES

- Methods for Grades 7 and 8
- Methods for Grades 5 and 6
- Methods for Grades 3 and 4
- Methods for Grades 1 and 2
- Introduction to the Learner
- The Role of the Catechist
- The Person of the Catechist
- Getting Started as a Catechist

Name

1.
2.
3.
4.
5.
6.
7.
8.
9.
10.
11.
12.
13.
14.
15.

APPENDIX F

This certifies that

_____
(name)

of

_____
(name of parish/school)

has completed

_____
(name of Echoes module)

on

_____
(date)

Signed

_____
(Catechetical Leader)